CONTENTS

2 – CHERYL AND THE GIRLS
8 – THE NATION'S SWEETHEART
10 – PRECOCIOUS CHILD
14 – POPSTAR TO SUPERSTAR
22 – MRS COLE
44 – SHE'S GOT THE X FACTOR
62 – GOING SOLO

A Mirror publication
Marketing Manager: Fergus McKenna
Mirrorpix: David Scripps and Alex Waters
020 7293 3858

Produced by Trinity Mirror Sport Media, PO BOX 48, Liverpool L69 3EB. 0151 227 2000

Executive Editor: Ken Rogers **Senior Editor:** Steve Hanrahan
Senior Art Editor: Rick Cooke **Editor:** Paul Dove
Compiled and written by: Alan Jewell **Sub Editor:** James Cleary
Design: Matthew Barnes
Part of the Mirror Collection © Published by Trinity Mirror
Images: Mirrorpix, Trinity Mirror, PA Photos
Printed by PCP

Discography

GIRLS ALOUD

Singles:

2002:
Sound of the Underground: UK No. 1

2003:
No Good Advice: UK No. 2
Life Got Cold: UK No. 3
Jump: UK No. 2

2004:
The Show: UK No. 2
Love Machine: UK No. 2
I'll Stand By You: UK No. 1

2005:
Wake Me Up: UK No. 4
Long Hot Summer: UK No. 7
Biology: UK No. 4
See The Day: UK No. 9

2006:
Whole Lotta History: UK No. 5
Something Kinda Ooooh: UK No. 3
I Think We're Alone Now: UK No. 4

2007:
Walk This Way (with Sugababes): UK No. 1
Sexy! No No No…: UK No. 5
Call The Shots: UK No. 3

2008:
Can't Speak French: UK No. 9
The Promise: UK No. 1

2009:
The Loving Kind: UK No. 10
Untouchable: UK No. 11

Albums:

Sound of the Underground (2003)

What Will the Neighbours Say? (2004)

Chemistry (2005)

The Sound of Girls Aloud (2006)

Tangled Up (2007)

Out of Control (2008)

SOLO CAREER

Singles:

2009:
Fight For This Love: UK No. 1
3 Words: UK No. 4

2010:
Parachute: UK No. 5
Promise This (Due to be released on October 25, 2010)

Albums:

3 Words (2009)

Messy Little Raindrops (Due to be released on November 1, 2010)

THE NATION'S SWEETHEART

No matter what life throws at her, Cheryl Cole fights on. Singer, dancer, TV personality and style icon, she is one of the most successful celebrities in Britain today

For someone who is only 27 years old, Cheryl Cole has experienced a very eventful life.

Despite experiencing a tough, no frills upbringing on Newcastle council estates, she is now a hugely successful singer, television personality and style icon.

Rich beyond her wildest dreams, it hasn't all been red carpets and roses for Cheryl. There has been plenty of anguish and heartache along the way.

Part of her popularity can be put down to her vulnerability: to how people can relate to her experiences, good and bad.

It's just eight years since the then teenage Cheryl Tweedy was catapulted to fame in the ITV talent contest Popstars: The Rivals.

She was the first girl chosen to be part of the group who became 'Girls Aloud'. Within weeks of their formation they had the Christmas number one single with 'Sound of the Underground'.

A dancer, singer and model as a child, appearing on Top of the Pops and having a chart-topping single were dreams fulfilled.

Cheryl was on top of the world but within weeks she was arrested after an altercation with a nightclub toilet attendant.

Charged with actual bodily harm and racially aggravated assault, she was eventually found guilty of ABH, while being cleared of the racial element.

She recovered from what was a traumatic experience and has since gone from strength to strength.

In 2004 she met footballer Ashley Cole and from that point her private life effectively ceased to exist.

They married in 2006 and the footballer-pop star combination was perfect for newspapers, celebrity magazines and gossip websites.

Their life together was a source of fascination to the media and every drama, big or small, was played out in public.

Cheryl adored Ashley but he wasn't loyal to her, cheating on her with a number of women. When more stories emerged about his infidelities early in 2010, she ended the marriage.

Since the split, she has become close to professional dancer Derek Hough, who has often been at her side during a period of immense strain.

Hough took her on holiday to Tanzania in June, a country she fell in love with while climbing Mount Kilimanjaro for Comic Relief in 2009. Shortly after returning to Britain, she collapsed during a photoshoot and was diagnosed with malaria. After resting for a few weeks, she was able to resume a full schedule.

Through all the turbulence and heartbreak, Cheryl has not allowed the distractions to cloud her career.

Girls Aloud are one of the most successful groups of all time. Between 2002 and 2009 they released 21 singles in the UK: four have reached number one, and all but one have reached the top 10. They have sold over 10 million records worldwide and all their albums have gone platinum. It has been an unbroken run of success.

After their Out of Control tour in 2009, the girls announced they were taking a break. As of October 2010, there are no firm plans for when they will work together again.

Of course, Cheryl has demonstrated that she is more than capable of forging ahead alone.

Her first solo album, '3 Words', went to number one, as did its lead single, 'Fight For This Love'. She has collaborated with will.i.am from the Black Eyes Peas in recent years, and supported his band during their European tour in 2010. Her second album, 'Messy Little Raindrops', was due to be released on November 1.

Since 2008 she has been a regular fixture on Saturday night TV as one of the judges on The X Factor. Her charm and ability to relate to the contestants has made her extremely popular with viewers. She mentored the winners in 2008 and 2009, Alexandra Burke and Joe McElderry. Fellow judge Simon Cowell has remarked: "She must now be the most popular person on TV."

The face of L'Oreal, her face regularly adorns the front cover of magazines such as Vogue, Elle, Hello, OK and even rock publication Q. In June 2010, Jo Elvin, editor of Glamour, described her as "the new Diana in terms of sales".

Cheryl has just released her first official book, 'Through My Eyes', which charts her rise to fame through photographs and personal memories. It's sure to be hugely popular, given her wide appeal amongst both sexes and across the age ranges.

What a story she has, and there's sure to be plenty more eventful and exciting chapters written in the future.

> "Cheryl has demonstrated that she is more than capable of forging ahead alone"

PRECOCIOUS CHILD

A young Geordie called Cheryl Tweedy was determined to make a name for herself. A singer and a dancer, this ambitious little girl was a natural performer from an early age

Above: A school photograph with brother Andrew

Opposite, bottom and this page: Cheryl, aged nine, was chosen to attend Royal Ballet School classes

Opposite page: With loving mum Joan, to whom she remains extremely close

Above & below: Bright lights and a microphone in hand, aged 13

CHERYL

POPSTAR TO
SUPERSTAR

The early 2000s saw a raft of reality TV contests hit the screens. Most of the acts disappeared as quickly as they arrived but that wasn't the case with the winners of Popstars: The Rivals. Cheryl Tweedy and Girls Aloud were here to stay

Above: The 'Buy Girls – Bye Boys' slogan worked: Girls Aloud thrashed their Popstars' rivals, One True Voice, in the race for the 2002 Christmas number one

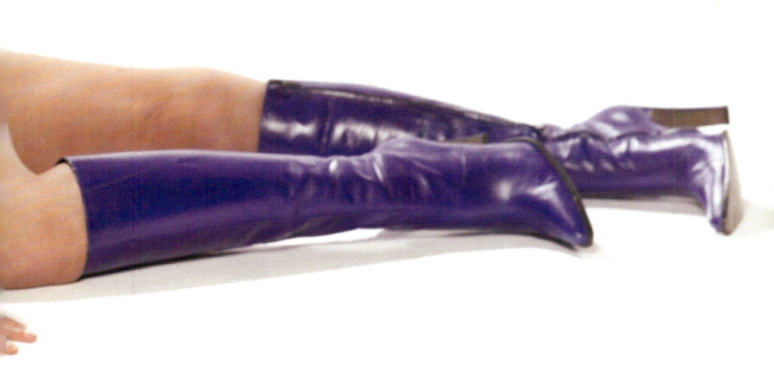

Above: Showing off the first Girls Aloud single, 'Sound of the Underground', at the HMV store in the Trafford Centre, Manchester

Christmas No. 1: The Rivals

Tuesday, December 17, 2002

Girl power looked to have the upper hand yesterday in the battle for the Christmas No. 1 slot.

Popstars: The Rivals group Girls Aloud moved ahead of the show's boy-band, One True Voice, as hot favourites.

The bookies originally backed the lads' ballad, 'Sacred Trust', but by last night they had switched to the girls' more catchy number, 'Sound of the Underground'.

Record stores reported brisk sales for both singles. But a spokesman for William Hill said: "Since the girls' single was released we have had hundreds of bets coming in. They've obviously got a huge amount of support and as far as we are concerned, they're certainly the most popular."

Girls Aloud are odds-on favourites at 2-7, with One True Voice trailing at 4-1.

The girls – Nadine Coyle, Cheryl Tweedy, Sarah Harding, Nicola Roberts and Kimberley Walsh – are said to be delighted with the response to their debut effort.

Industry insiders reckon the girls will pip the boys to the post. "They've simply got a better song," said one.

No. 1 and we can't stop screaming

Monday, December 23, 2002

Girls Aloud last night won the battle to be top of the pops this Christmas.

The group from TV's Popstars: the Rivals beat boy-band One True Voice to the No. 1 spot with their single 'Sound of the Underground'.

Singer Nicola Roberts, 17, said last night: "We can't stop screaming. This is the perfect Christmas present."

The group flogged 213,000 copies of their single. One True Voice's track, 'Sacred Trust', sold 147,000.

Nicola, and the rest of the girls – Nadine Coyle, Sarah Harding, Cheryl Tweedy and Kimberley Walsh – said they would "party all over Christmas" to celebrate.

Cheryl, 19, said: "This is more than we ever expected. It's been an exhausting few weeks but worth it."

The battle for this year's Christmas number one spot has been particularly bitter.

Last week, One True Voice manager Pete Waterman accused the girls of not even singing on their debut track and claimed they had used session musicians.

He said: "It's a smashing pop record, but they're not on it."

But Girls Aloud boss Louis Walsh insisted the five do sing on the single and branded One True Voice a "Westlife tribute band".

The girls show their joy at becoming the Christmas No. 1 in 2002

Cheryl on her mum, Joan:

"My mum is more like a friend. I can talk to her about anything – boyfriends, sex – and we go out together to a lot of clubs. We get dressed up and have a right laugh.

"But she has got a serious side, too. She had her first baby at 17, so she had to grow up fast and with five of us to look after she had to work hard.

"Whatever happens with the band, I'm going to make sure she is looked after. When I decided I wanted to make a go of it as a singer she spent a lot of time making my outfits and driving me about to the dance studios. At the same time she told me that showbiz can be tough and I had to be prepared to take the rejections. She is a very positive, independent person at the end of the day and I think that's rubbed off on me."

Celebrating the most exciting Christmas of her life with mum Joan, at home in Newcastle

CHERYL

Fresh-faced young girls ready to take the charts by storm

'Cheryl guilty'

Tuesday, October 21, 2003

Girls Aloud star Cheryl Tweedy was yesterday cleared of being a racist – but found guilty of an assault on a toilet attendant.

It took the jury under three hours to convict Tweedy of assault occasioning actual bodily harm on Sophie Amogbokpa, 39.

But she was cleared of racially aggravated ABH. The 20-year-old had claimed she hit Mrs Amogbokpa in self-defence in a club in Guildford, Surrey.

The jury at Kingston Crown Court agreed there was no racial element to the attack, but the singer held her head as they found her guilty of ABH.

Tweedy was given 120 hours' community service, ordered to pay £500 compensation and £3,000 costs.

Judge Richard Haworth said: "It was an unpleasant piece of violence which caused Sophie Amogbokpa pain. She had bruising and blurred vision."

In a statement, read by her solicitor Paul Harris outside court, Tweedy said: "I am stunned by the conviction for assault."

Arriving at Kingston Crown Court during her trial in October 2003

Receiving the Band of the Year award at a Glamour magazine ceremony in 2004

Below: Showing her style at a childrens' charity event in April 2004

On stage during the Live 'N' Loud concert at Hampden Park, June 2004

őt
Mrs Cole

Cheryl had not long celebrated her 21st birthday when she met the man of her dreams, footballer Ashley Cole. Less than two years later they were married. For a time she was blissfully happy – but there was trouble ahead. Despite the turmoil in her not-so-private life, her singing career went from strength to strength

Goals aloud

Thursday, November 25, 2004

Girls Aloud star Cheryl Tweedy has opened her heart about Arsenal player Ashley Cole, on the eve of their one-month anniversary.

Which, let's face it, is a long time in showbiz.

Speaking for the first time about their romance, the 21-year-old Geordie told us yesterday: "Things are really good between us.

"He makes me very happy and puts a big smile on my face."

We bet he does.

And that's not all Cheryl's got to smile about – the latest Girls Aloud single, 'I'll Stand by You', is on course to be at number one for the second week.

Cheryl got it together with the hunky England international at Funky Buddha on October 26.

Earlier, Girls Aloud had been presenters at the National Television Awards before she and a few others headed off to the West End club.

She and Ashley were bumping and grinding on the dancefloor in no time.

He is not Cheryl's first footballing fella. She had a few dates with Newcastle's Kieron Dyer last year. That went nowhere, but this could stay the course.

Because she and Ashley happen to live in the same block of flats in North London, their relationship has been able to blossom away from prying eyes.

He's even met her mum, Joan, when she stayed last week in the flat Cheryl shares with her bandmate Nicola Roberts.

"My mam really approves of him," she said.

They may be a celebrity couple, but Cheryl and Ashley have been extremely surreptitious about their dates. In fact, they've hardly left his £750,000 penthouse.

Left: A radiant smile while attending the 2005 Brit Awards

Below and opposite page: Posing at a Girls Aloud photoshoot in February 2005

Cheryl's premier romance

Monday, February 21, 2005

It must be hard not to seem smug when there's a £50,000-a-week England footballer scattering rose petals on your bed.

Not to mention pouring you champagne and preparing your scented, candlelit bath.

But for Cheryl Tweedy, the extravagantly romantic Valentine's Day gesture by boyfriend Ashley Cole was a reason to recognise how much her life has changed in 18 months.

Then, the Girls Aloud beauty was at rock bottom after being found guilty of attacking a toilet attendant in a nightclub. Her career hung in the balance and she had no boyfriend to share the pain. Today she has put the conviction behind her, Girls Aloud is the top girl band and she is blissfully in love.

Life, says Cheryl, could not be any better.

"I've never been this happy," she smiles. "The past year has been the best. I feel like I've got a fairy godmother watching over me."

Ashley and Cheryl are inseparable. She breaks into a huge smile at the mention of his name.

"I've never been in a relationship like this where I've been treated like a princess," she says.

"Valentine's Day was beautiful. Ashley ran a lovely bath with bubbles and candles and rose petals everywhere. He bought champagne and chocolate. It was really magical and he wrote the most gorgeous words in my card.

"This is all new to me. I keep thinking that there must be something wrong with him. I know I shouldn't think that, but I just can't help it."

In 2003 it was a very different story. The pop dream Cheryl had worked so hard to achieve threatened to become a nightmare when she was found guilty of attacking toilet attendant Sophie Amogbokpa in a Guildford nightclub.

Cheryl, it was alleged, lashed out at her over an argument over a lollipop.

Afterwards, she said: "The worst thing was to be labelled a racist. Anyone who knows me knows that's so far from the truth. I find it insulting."

The second youngest of five children, Cheryl always wanted to be an entertainer.

Before being picked to be in the band, she did endless auditions and showcases but a recording contract proved elusive.

"I used to enter loads of dance competitions," she says. "I got into the Royal Ballet's White Lodge Academy and I wrote loads of songs. My dad used to say: 'You need to get your head out of the clouds.'

"When I went home after getting in the band, my family threw me a surprise party. My dad said: 'I told her to go to college and have something to fall back on and she said I would be eating humble pie when she got on Top of the Pops. I have to say I'm eating a big slice of it now.'"

The band – formed on ITV show Popstars: The Rivals in late 2002 – are one of the few manufactured bands still going strong.

Cheryl puts part of their success down to their wide appeal. "We appeal to younger girls because we're fun-loving and they can copy our dances," she says. "Students can identify with us as normal lasses falling out of nightclubs or getting p***** and making mistakes."

She finds it hard to believe everything is going so well.

"Sometimes I yearn to wake up and be in my mum's house and see my little dogs, but then I remind myself that I'm doing what thousands of young girls dream of doing."

With the girls as they are named Best UK Act at the 2005 TMF Awards

Proud to be aloud
Tuesday, June 14, 2005

She may be dating England footie star Ashley Cole but if you tell Cheryl Tweedy that she's a typical trophy girlfriend, she'll show you the red card.

The Girls Aloud star said: "It really annoys me when people try to call me a footballer's wife. Footballers' wives have no career and live off their husband's money.

"I was in Girls Aloud before I met Ashley and have my own successful career. I'm not going to quit the band and sit around in the sun all day or go shopping with Ashley's plastic.

"If I'm going shopping I'll pay with the money I have worked hard for."

In fact, 21-year-old Cheryl hates the label so much that when she was approached recently to take part in a footballers' girlfriends' photoshoot for Vogue, she refused.

She dismissed reports that she is on the verge of quitting the band.

"I'm not leaving the band, that is absolute rubbish. Why am I going to walk away from Girls Aloud? We have just finished our sell-out tour and our last album went double platinum. We're having an amazing time right now."

Left: Looking stunning at the 2005 Daily Mirror Pride of Britain Awards

Opposite: Cheryl and Ashley are named Hottest Showbiz Couple at the T4 Poll Winners Party, November 2005

We're Gunner be wed

Friday, June 17, 2005

Girls Aloud star Cheryl Tweedy is engaged to Arsenal and England defender Ashley Cole.

Ashley got down on one knee and proposed to the Geordie singer while they were on holiday in Dubai.

He presented her with a £50,000 diamond ring and Cheryl, who told us earlier in the week that she hated being thought of as a footballers' wife, accepted at once.

"Ashley's proposal came as a complete surprise to Cheryl," says our source. "They've only been dating for nine months but are totally inseparable and madly in love."

Ashley, 24, whisked 21-year-old Cheryl away on a luxury break in Dubai 10 days ago after she finished the Girls Aloud sell-out tour.

The couple jetted back to London on Wednesday and yesterday afternoon flew to Newcastle so they could show off the ring to her family and friends."

Cheryl's mum, Joan, told us last night: "We are all delighted for her. Ashley is a lovely lad and we could not be happier for the two of them. They are such a lovely couple."

Cheryl and Ashley are understood to be heading to Spain to celebrate their engagement.

I'm going maid!

Thursday, December 15, 2005

Expect an almighty scrum when Cheryl Tweedy flings her bouquet at her wedding guests – because there will be so many bridesmaids scrabbling to catch it.

The 22-year-old Girls Aloud stunner, who is to marry Arsenal ace Ashley Cole in July, is so desperate not to offend anyone that she could be followed down the aisle by an army of helpers.

"I've got a family who will never talk to me again if they're not bridesmaids," Cheryl told us at the Help A London Child 30th anniversary bash at London's Trocadero on Tuesday.

"And my bandmates would probably not forgive me if they don't get to follow me up the aisle, too.

"I can't have 10 bridesmaids but I don't want to let anyone down. It's doing my head in, to be honest."

Still, she is not letting this dilemma ruin the build-up to her big day. "I'm so excited about getting married," she said. "I want a huge meringue wedding dress.

"It's a tough choice between a fairytale one or a sleek one. I always thought I'd go for something more demure, but this is my big day so I'm going to go for it. I've already started looking – it's so exciting."

This page: Girls Aloud attend a Christmas party in 2005

Girls elope

Tuesday, April 4, 2006

Cheryl Tweedy admitted last night she is stressed out over plans for her showbiz wedding to soccer ace Ashley Cole – and wishes they could just run away together.

The Girls Aloud singer said of the arrangements for the lavish bash in August: "It's seriously stressful – it's like another full-time job.

"I've hired a wedding planner but all he ever does is call me and ask me to make more decisions. I feel like I'm living with a phone glued to my ear.

"Right now I'm starting to think I should jack it all in and Ashley and I should run off and elope somewhere.

"I just want it to be him and me, alone on a beach – but I know my mum would kill me if I did."

Cheryl, 22, poured her heart out as she arrived with Arsenal star Ashley, 25, and 24-year-old band-mate Kimberley Walsh for the London premiere of Ant and Dec's debut movie, 'Alien Autopsy'.

Above: With Ashley at the premiere of 'Alien Autopsy', Leicester Square, London, April 2006

CHERYL

Cheryl arrives at Baden-Baden airport before the World Cup began. It was during this tournament that the term 'WAGs' caught on, as the wives and girlfriends of the England players partied and shopped

Leaving a restaurant in Baden-Baden, Germany, with Victoria Beckham during the 2006 World Cup. Inset, with Coleen McLoughlin

WAGs at war

Tuesday, June 27, 2006

It's being dubbed the war of the WAGs and the action is almost as gripping as watching our boys on the pitch.

England's glamorous wives and girlfriends are locked in a desperate battle for attention — and this game is definitely going to extra-time.

From their designer outfits to competitive shopping bouts, the girls' attempts at outdoing each other seem to know no bounds.

Sources at the group's luxury hotel in Baden-Baden have claimed the atmosphere is "not unlike a blinged-up Big Brother".

The insider explained: "The WAGs are all exhibitionists who know they're on camera. At first it was all nicey-nice but then their characters start to show. The competitiveness and bitching is growing ever more intense."

At the top of the tree in the WAGs' world are Nancy Dell'Olio and Victoria Beckham, 32.

Victoria is said to be keen to distance herself from any back-biting. The insider added: "She's been in this game for years. She's got decorum. Some of the others couldn't even spell the word."

Concerns are also being raised about the girls' boozy antics. "Nancy and Victoria think it's a bit out of hand and that some have forgotten why they're out in Germany.

"It's like an all-night, all-day downmarket hen do. All they need is the L-plates."

Ashley Cole's fiancée, Cheryl Tweedy, has become very close to Posh. The source said: "Cheryl doesn't understand girls whose lives revolve around shopping, especially with their partner's money. Coleen McLoughlin is also friendly with Cheryl and Posh and she's down-to-earth."

CHERYL

Opposite: Hand in hand with Ashley, after England had beaten Ecuador
Above: Watching the quarter-final against Portugal, which England lost on penalties. The picture on the right shows a consoling hug between Cheryl, Victoria and David Beckham's mother, Sandra

CHERYL

Say cheesy!
Wednesday, July 12, 2006

Oh no, not another embarrassing performance by an England star…

Ashley Cole does a great impersonation of Medallion Man in this cheesy pose with fiancée Cheryl Tweedy.

The 25-year-old Arsenal defender looks more like Lenny Henry's comic soul star Theophilus P Wildebeest than a Premier League footballer. And Cheryl, 23, could be auditioning for a part in a Barbie movie.

The couple, who are getting married on Saturday, dolled up to launch the National Lottery's new Dream Number game. Cheryl gushed: "I've found my dream match. Ashley is one in a million." He added: "It's great that there's another big game to watch."

DAILY MIRROR, Saturday, July 15, 2006 — PAGE 3

WAGs' WEDDING OF THE YEAR

Ssshampagne Sssheryl

WHAT A BELTER: Cheryl in good voice

EXCLUSIVE
By SARAH TETTEH

GIRLS Aloud star Cheryl Tweedy collapsed in a nightclub during her boozy hen night before the Wags' wedding of the year.

The stunning singer, who marries England footballer Ashley Cole today, had been knocking back pink champagne and vodka cocktails into the early hours of yesterday morning.

She cracked her head on stairs in her fall during a wild night in which Cheryl, 23, and her band-mates danced on the tables.

Besides drinking, they excitedly inhaled flavoured tobacco from a bubbling Egyptian shisha water pipe. At one stage Cheryl sang into the pipe, pretending it was a microphone.

The 15-strong party kicked off their mega knees-up just before midnight when they arrived unannounced at the top Umbaba nightclub in the West End of London.

A witness said: "Cheryl ended up so drunk that when Nicola rushed over to hug her she collapsed and hit her head on a few steps.

"The pair just lay there giggling. It took four people to drag her up but then she reached for

WAGs TO RICHES: CHERYL'S STORY
PAGES 22 AND 23

even more champers. Afterwards she panicked about having bruises on her wedding day."

Cheryl told The Mirror: "I keep thinking I'm going to trip up the aisle. But I have to remember to be elegant. I have to glide."

Revellers included Cheryl's mum Joan and band-mates Nicola Roberts, 20, Nadine Coyle, 21, Sarah Harding, 24 and Kimberley Walsh, also 24, who organised the evening.

At one stage Nicola had cross words with a toilet attendant who told her to hurry up.

Nicola barked: "What are you talking about? I've got to do my make-up."

Sarah stepped in to calm the situation down but the incident had alarming echoes of Cheryl's row with a toilet attendant in 2003. She was found guilty of assault and was sentenced to 120 hours of community service.

On their way out, plastered Cheryl, Kimberley and Nicola performed a rendition of I'm Getting Married In The Morning.

Cheryl looked bemused when a passer-by asked her to marry him. As the girls climbed into their car she mumbled: "Where is he?"

If she meant Ashley, he had been tucked up in bed for hours after a dinner with close pals near his home in Cockfosters, North London.

Kerber and Black: Page 8

sarah.tetteh@mirror.co.uk

FUN TIME: Kim, Cheryl and Nicola

FIZZ FAN: Bubbly for Cheryl, left, with Nicola, centre

HEN PECK: Sarah, left, and Nicola embracing Cheryl

QUEEZY: Cheryl, left, as Nadine laughs

Above: Cheryl and the girls enjoy a drunken hen night before her wedding to Ashley Cole

CHERYL

"She has wanted to be a star since she was a child. She didn't want to do anything else. Nothing else would have satisfied her"

Right: The Daily Mirror looks at Cheryl's background on the day she married Ashley Cole

EXCLUSIVE
By DOUG WATSON

AS a sweet-faced six-year-old in a frilly pink outfit with her hair tied up in bunches, Cheryl Tweedy won £150 worth of clothing vouchers in a newspaper competition.

Today, the singer from the back streets of Newcastle who found fame in Girls Aloud will be wearing a bridal gown that costs nearly one thousand times that amount.

As 23-year-old Cheryl walks down the aisle to marry her soccer star sweetheart Ashley Cole, 25, in what is being called the WAG wedding of the year, she will look stunning in a £110,000 dress.

It was created by Roberto Cavalli – the favourite designer of her new best friend Victoria Beckham – at a private sitting in Milan.

And the guest-list for the £1.5million nuptials at Highclere Castle in Berkshire is a glittering Who's Who of showbiz and football celebrities.

It's all a world away from the tough council estate on Tyneside where she grew up. And from the very beginning the ambitious youngster hasn't let anything stand in her way – not even romance.

As she fought through the public vote on ITV's Popstars: The Rivals to land a place in chart-topping band Girls Aloud, Cheryl dumped her boyfriend Richard Sweeney.

She had been working as a £5 an hour cocktail waitress on Tyneside's floating nightclub Tuxedo Princess when her romance with Richard began.

A former friend of the couple recalls: "He was totally smitten with Cheryl and thought they had a future together. They were both from working-class Geordie backgrounds and shared a love of music.

"But when Cheryl auditioned for Popstars and finally knew her big break was about to happen, she broke it off with him.

"She has always been determined to be a star and Richard was no longer part of her plans. He was heartbroken but there was nothing he could do. That was nearly four years ago but he still carries a torch for her and won't hear a bad word said against her.

"Their relationship still comes back to haunt him. Whenever he switched on the telly to watch an England match in the World Cup there was Cheryl's face on the screen – smiling and waving as she sat beside Posh, looking like the queen bee.

"She hurt him very badly but he doesn't blame her. He would have loved her to become Mrs Sweeney instead of Mrs Cole. Her wedding day will be hard for him."

RICHARD is reluctant to talk about their doomed love affair and has turned down big-money offers for a kiss-and-tell.

But he told the Daily Mirror: "Cheryl is a lovely girl. She has always wanted to be where she is now. She has been through some rough times and now she is living her dream. I wish her all the best."

Cheryl's love of the limelight began when she was only three and won a string of bonny baby competitions. As a seven-year-old she was a child model and appeared in TV commercials for British Gas and a fashion chain.

Her mum Joan recalls: "From the age of four she went to shopping centres all over the place, strutting her stuff on catwalks and stages.

"She has wanted to be a star since she was a child. She didn't want to do anything else. Nothing else would have satisfied her."

Growing up in the Newcastle suburb of Heaton with her brothers Joseph, Andrew and Gary and sister Gillian, the family budget was tight.

But dad Gary, a painter and decorator, always found the money to send Cheryl to auditions.

Her former headmaster at the inner-city Walker School, Dr Steve Gater recalls: "It was obvious early on that Cheryl was ambitious and talented. From a young age her passions were singing and dancing. The staff didn't anticipate how big she would become but clearly the potential was there.

"She stood head and shoulders above everybody else. She loved being centre stage. Once she gave a speech to 250 kids for a Christmas Box appeal and was so good that a letter of commendation was sent to her parents."

Eager to sharpen her talent, Cheryl took lessons at the Newcastle Dance Centre when she was 10. She doubled up with a boy partner for the British Dance Championships and performed with him on Michael Barrymore's prime-time Saturday night TV show.

She returned to the Centre in her teens to have dance routines choreographed, before singing solo to shoppers at the MetroCentre in Gateshead.

TUTU MUCH: At Royal Ballet school

DREAMING OF FAME: Aged seven

AMBITIOUS: Cheryl strikes a pose

WAGS WEDDING OF THE YEAR

DAILY MIRROR, Saturday, July 15, 2006 — PAGE 23

Cheryl's PERILS

The obstacles on her rise from a tough Tyneside council estate to finding fame with Girls Aloud

CUTE: The smile that won Cheryl a Bonny Baby competition

IN LOVE: Cheryl and Ashley will get hitched today

INSIDE: Brother Andrew

The Centre's principal, Michael Conway, says: "Cheryl always wanted to be a star. She had charisma and lots of talent but she also worked very hard to learn her routines. Everyone here is proud of what she's achieved."

But it wasn't all plain sailing. When she was nine years old, she was one of a handful of girls chosen out of 5,000 to audition for the Royal Ballet's summer school. She hated it.

Cheryl says: "I wanted to go home straight away. Everyone was prim and proper and I was just a Geordie from a council estate. Their parents all had money and we struggled just to get the cash to travel down to London. I felt that I was the odd one out."

She trained for two weeks but cried herself to sleep at night because she was homesick. So she decided she didn't want to be a ballerina after all. "It shattered my dream but I didn't want to have to stand a certain way all my life and only eat salad," she says.

Even when she found the fame she craved when Girls Aloud's debut single, Sound Of The Underground, hit the Christmas No.1 spot in 2002, she faced several setbacks.

In January 2003 she feared her pop career was over when she punched a toilet attendant in a booze-fuelled rage during a night out with bandmate Nicola Roberts at he Drink club in Guildford, Surrey.

Cheryl was charged with racially aggravated assault after allegedly calling 39-year-old Sophie Amogbokpa "a f***ing black bitch." She spent a night in a police cell because she was too drunk to be interviewed.

In October 2003, she was cleared of being racist but convicted of assault and sentenced to 120 hours community service plus £3,000 prosecution costs for what the judge called "an unpleasant piece of drunken violence".

Back home on Tyneside, Cheryl began her community work, sandpapering benches at a local football ground and picking up litter – her expensive designer handbag slung over her shoulder. Shortly after her arrest, she was kicked out of a nightclub following a water pistol fight with some Newcastle United players.

Also earlier that year, revelations about her 26-year-old brother Andrew – an alcoholic who is also addicted to sniffing glue – threatened to overshadow her success. He has a criminal record of more than 70 offences that began when he was 13 and includes convictions for robbery, assault and attacking police officers. He is currently serving four years for a vicious street mugging.

She wanted to be a star.. nothing else

BUT since she started dating 25-year-old Arsenal left-back Ashley in October 2004, Cheryl has put her troubles behind her.

She says: "I don't really go out much any more. I can't be bothered and I'm not a very good drinker. I used to love going to parties and clubs but I think I've grown out of it now. It doesn't interest me."

She certainly distanced herself from the boozy antics of the WAGs during the World Cup, finding an ally in Posh.

While the others partied, they finalised wedding plans. Because the wedding is being covered by a glossy magazine, everyone attending has had to sign a confidentiality document. A special clause forbids guest from approaching any of the celebs with a request for autographs.

Those stars will include footballers Rio Ferdinand and Jermaine Jenas, who also attended Ashley's £30,000 stag do in the Costa del Sol. Plus, of course, Cheryl's bandmates.

Cheryl, who once vowed that she would never date a footballer, knows just how lucky she is. Not only has she dragged herself from obscurity to find fame with the biggest girl band since the Spice Girls, but she is marrying the man of her dreams.

Today, as the bubbly flows and she watches her working-class family mingle with the rich and famous, it will be another reminder of how far she has come from the little girl of six who won the Star Of The Future contest in her local newspaper.

features@mirror.co.uk

Above: The girls performing in November 2006

Cheryl's tears at dad's plea

Wednesday, July 17, 2006

Cheryl Tweedy – oops, Cole – wiped away tears as her dad pleaded with his new son-in-law not to take his "little girl" away.

Amid rumours of footballer Ashley's imminent move to Spain, Geordie Gary Tweedy used the WAG wedding of the year to make an emotional plea for the newlyweds to stay in Britain.

One guest whispered to us: "Gary got quite emotional and said that when Cheryl joined Girls Aloud it felt like he had lost his little girl. Gary then pleaded that if she and Ashley move abroad, it would be like losing her again. Cheryl then appeared and they had an emotional hug."

Cheryl, 23, and Ashley, 25, tied the knot in secret at Sopwell House Hotel in St Albans, Herts, on Friday.

But it was at the high-security £500,000 reception at nearby Wrotham Park on Saturday – where camera-shy Cheryl rolled up in a horse-drawn carriage with blacked-out windows – that Cheryl's decorator dad got all emotional.

And the Newcastle United fan – who started his speech with the Toon's typical "why aye man" greeting – couldn't resist having a pop at Ashley's current team Arsenal.

Cheryl's band-mates Sarah Harding, Nadine Coyle, Kimberley Walsh and Nicola Roberts – dressed in burnt orange dresses with a zebra print hem – all had tears in their eyes as he cooed: "When Cheryl was born I was holding this bundle of joy in my hands but now Ashley has come and made her the happiest woman in the world. Now I want him to make me the happiest man in the world by accepting this gift."

And everyone – especially Ashley's England team-mates Sol Campbell and Jermaine Jenas – cracked up laughing as he whipped out a Newcastle United shirt with Cole on the back.

"Come on Ashley – make my dream come true," he added. "On second thoughts you better give that to Cheryl to wear when she comes to see the Toon Army play because she's Cheryl Cole now."

Above: Performing with Girls Aloud at the T4 Party on the Beach festival, Weston-super-Mare, July 2007

Smash hit for Cheryl

Thursday, May 17, 2007

As pop feuds go, it's like Tyson vs Holyfield. Loudmouth Lily Allen has had Cheryl Cole on the ropes with her bitchy insults – but now our girl Chezza is hitting back…

On Tuesday, 22-year-old Lily really punched below the belt. During an interview with E! Radio in the States, she lashed out, branding the Girls Aloud babe "thick", "disgusting" and poking fun at her accent.

Ex-public schoolgirl Lily sniped of her rival: "I hate her guts. She's a horrible, nasty, disgusting human being."

Attempting to mimic Cheryl's dulcet Tyneside tones, she scoffed: "She has a really stupid accent."

Unsurprisingly, the gloves are now off and 24-year-old Cheryl has come out fighting. She insists that Lily would never come close to her own chart success of 15 top 10 hits.

And she dodges that sneering blow about her Geordie accent by saying: "I'd like to see her step foot in Newcastle now – she's the dumb one."

For a round-up of the ringside action so far…Lily threw the first punch by sniping about Cheryl's hubby Ashley Cole and her bandmates. That sparked Cheryl to retort on Gordon Ramsey's The F Word that Lily was a "chick with a d***".

Now Cheryl tells us: "I couldn't care less if she has a d*** or not. I have had enough of her and her big mouth.

"Over the last few months she has called Nicola ugly, Sarah vile and my husband horrendous. I can't stand people who give it but aren't prepared to take it.

"She should keep her mouth shut instead of feeling sorry for herself. I left school a long time ago and I have no time for this.

"I'm currently on a big arena tour with the girls, singing live each night. Lily, I could find you a ticket if you'd like to see a live arena tour – as it's the closest you'll get."

CHERYL

CHERYL

From CAROLINE HEDLEY in Los Angeles

SHE might be married to a footballing hero but you take your life in your hands if you dare call Cheryl Cole a WAG.

Fiercely independent and hard-working, the Geordie firebrand pays her own way as a singer with Girls Aloud and recently returned a Bentley that her husband Ashley Cole bought her because she felt she hadn't earned it.

No wonder she is sickened by women who see bagging themselves a rich Premiership footballer as a career option. Not that she fears Ashley, a Chelsea and England defender, would ever succumb to their dubious charms.

Speaking exclusively to the Mirror, Cheryl says: "I know there are a lot of desperate girls out there who want to get themselves a footballer.

"I just think it's funny that anyone could be that pathetic. I know Ashley, and I know that nothing like that would affect us. It's embarrassing and depressing when I hear kids say to me, 'I wanna be a WAG'. That's not a job!"

Cheryl has been in Los Angeles to film a documentary, and there is a possibility she may bump into one wannabe WAG she particularly loathes – Rebecca Loos.

Her good friend Victoria Beckham recently admitted that Rebecca's allegations of having an affair with David, while he was playing for Real Madrid, put a strain on their marriage, saying: "It was a really tough time. It was hard for our entire families."

So the news that Rebecca was planning to follow the Beckhams to Los Angeles made 24-year-old Cheryl's blood boil.

"That Rebecca Loos, I really, really hate her," she says. "I couldn't believe she'd try and do that. How dare she try and upset them!

"Anyone who knows them can see how happy and in love they are. Victoria's an incredible woman – a fashion icon, business-woman and a great wife and mother. David just dotes on her.

"That Rebecca just wants to peddle lies and bulls***. I don't know how she sleeps at night.

"What is she famous for? She's made a career from trying to destroy someone's marriage. She's the lowest of the low. And she just won't go away.

"I WAS at a party recently and she turned up. I was so furious that I had to leave or I'd have had to say something to her.

"I didn't want to embarrass the host so I just walked out. But it was hard to not give her a piece of my mind."

Speaking by the pool of the hip Standard Hotel in Los Angeles, Cheryl has her phone close by to keep up with texts from Ashley back home in England.

The couple tied the knot in a lavish £500,000 ceremony in Wrotham Park, Herts, in July 2006. And although Cheryl moans about Ashley's ineptitude around their Surrey home ("He rang me one day and asked, 'How do I cook SuperNoodles?'") it's clear their honeymoon period is far from over.

They are so close that at times like this, when they are apart, they run up huge phone bills talking and texting one another dozens of times a day.

"We are really, really happy", says Cheryl with a smile. "We spend every minute that we can together. He's not into showbiz parties or flashy restaurants, he just likes staying at home with me.

"At times I think I'd like to go to The Ivy or somewhere really trendy. But Ashley's not bothered about the whole celebrity thing. He's just an amazing, genuine man."

As she talks she toys with her diamond-encrusted watch – one gift from Ashley that she didn't return. "It's

CURVE APPEAL Cheryl shows off her stunning figure and, above, with Ashley in Lotto ad

STEPPING UP: With Girls Aloud

Right: Cheryl has never embraced the 'WAG' lifestyle

COLE EXCLUSIVE

It depresses me when kids say 'I want to be a WAG'. It's not a job!

massive, isn't it?", she says, looking slightly embarrassed. "It was a birthday present. He spent ages choosing it."

They would like to start a family but out of loyalty to Girls Aloud Cheryl has put baby plans on hold to fulfil her commitments with the band.

"I do really want a baby and so does Ashley, but it's not just my life I have to think about – there are five other people who would be affected if I got pregnant," she says.

"The band have got a bit of a break next year, once our tour is out of the way, so maybe then.

"There's so many things to consider, it's crazy. Like, if Ashley has a match on the day the baby is born, he still has to play, so he could miss the birth. We'll have to plan it with military precision."

At least when she does become a mum she will have four willing babysitters in her bandmates Sarah Harding, Kimberley Walsh, Nicola Roberts and Nadine Coyle.

The girls – who have notched up a record-breaking 16 consecutive Top 10 hits and over 4.2 million record sales in the UK alone – are currently filming a series of Passions documentaries for ITV2 on subjects close to their hearts. Cheryl's programme is on street dance, which is why she is here in Los Angeles, bringing her mum Joan along for the ride.

The film project has taken her to some of the roughest parts of the city, including Compton which is a hotbed for gang violence. But she insists she wasn't intimidated.

"I am so happy that I chose this as my documentary subject," she says. "I was going to do it on ballet as I trained as a ballerina,

I really hate Rebecca Loos – she's made a career out of trying to ruin a marriage

but I thought this would be more original.

"I can honestly say it has changed my life. It was a bit scary going into some of these neighbourhoods.

"People say you shouldn't drive through certain areas as you can get shot. I just put on jeans and trainers and took off my engagement ring and I didn't get any hassle at all. Some of the dancers I met were so talented but they've had tough lives. It was an incredible thing to be a part of."

A huge fan of Britney Spears, Cheryl was also hoping to meet the beleaguered singer during her stay.

"Nicola and I love her," she says. "I was desperate to run into her in LA. She's an icon and it's really sad what she's going through. She needs her family around her, people who can tell her what's real. I hope her mum makes her go to rehab. She can clean herself up, get her boys back and start making amazing music again."

With that her phone chimes with another message from Ashley. "I could extend my stay for a few days, Mum would love it" she says. "But I really want to get back to my husband."

●GIRLS Aloud's new single, Call The Shots, will be released on November 26.

caroline.hedley@mirror.co.uk

LOATHED: Loos

WE GOT INTO DEBT TO LIVE LIKE WAGS *Your*LIFE **pages 40 & 41**

Cheryl's just stunned by his betrayal... they were even talking about having a baby soon

Saturday, January 26, 2008

Friends of Cheryl Cole said she is absolutely devastated by husband Ashley's cheating – and feels utterly betrayed because they have been making plans to start a family.

One friend said: "Cheryl is in total shock. She thought she had found the man of her dreams in Ashley. But now those dreams have been crushed.

"The worst thing about it all was that it was totally unexpected. She is angry, but mostly stunned by his betrayal.

"No one can believe Ashley has done this to Cheryl. Everyone thought their relationship was rock solid and are as shocked as Cheryl is. It is a horrible, horrible mess."

Chelsea and England star Ashley bedded single mum Aimee Walton before Christmas at a friend's flat after meeting her at a West End nightclub while drunkenly celebrating a Premiership victory.

But stunned Cheryl, 24, only learned of his infidelity on Thursday after Aimee, a 22-year-old blonde hairdresser, sold her sordid story. The Girls Aloud singer spent a sleepless night rowing with the 27-year-old defender at their £3.5 million home in Oxshott, Surrey, following the revelations.

Finally she ordered him to temporarily move out of the house – saying she "needed some time" to think about the future of their 18-month marriage.

Cheryl's sense of betrayal has been fuelled by the fact that she and Ashley have recently been discussing trying for a baby next year.

Her friend added: "Cheryl needs to make some difficult decisions about her future.

"She's got some serious thinking to do. She has always been very outspoken on the subject of infidelity.

"Now she has to decide whether she wants to stay with Ashley or end their marriage.

"She has been through a lot of bad relationships where the men have treated her badly.

"She had no idea this news was about to break and she is utterly devastated. She has always been happy for him to go out with his mates and other footballers. She never worried about what he was getting up to as she had total faith in him, 100 per cent trust."

Cheryl and Ashley were at home together when they learned that Aimee was cashing in on her drunken romp. Ashley broke down in tears as furious Cheryl ripped into him.

The friend said: "Ashley was crying and begging for her forgiveness and promised her it was a one-off. Cheryl was crying too. But it is difficult to see where they go from here."

Ashley was late for football training yesterday – turning up at 11.30, a full hour after teammates Frank Lampard and John Terry. He had left home looking tired and sheepish but still wearing his diamond-encrusted platinum wedding ring.

The former Arsenal left-back later prepared to head to the North-West for today's televised FA Cup clash against Wigan.

Cheryl was consoled yesterday by mum Joan, who was already on a visit from the family's home in Byker, Newcastle. She is expected to stay with Cheryl over the weekend. Girls Aloud band members Nicola Roberts and Kimberley Walsh also phoned to comfort her.

Cheryl has been taking a break from her Girls Aloud duties over Christmas and is due to begin work again next week.

Girls Aloud, minus Nadine, attending the Brit Awards in 2008

Girls' night out

Thursday, February 21, 2008

Stunning Cheryl Cole opted for a big night out with the girls rather than a sad night in with her cheating hubby Ashley last night.

Wearing a broad smile and a canary yellow mini dress, Cheryl stole the show on the Brit Awards red carpet last night.

The Girls Aloud singer only decided to attend last night's ceremony as she and her band-mates made their way to LAX airport.

After her LA trip and a therapeutic beach holiday in Thailand, the 24-year-old star refused to confront love-rat Ashley when she touched down in London. Instead, she left the Chelsea defender to stew, postponing their crisis talks following the revelation that he cheated on her.

She said: "The holiday was fantastic, just what I needed. I feel great being back with the girls, but it's so much colder in London than it is in LA. I'm out to have some fun and really looking forward to it."

Cheat Cole back

Friday, February 22, 2008

Oh no! It's the news we all feared. Cheryl Cole yesterday took husband Ashley back after they met for the first time since his cheating was exposed three weeks ago.

She told her Girls Aloud band-mates at the Brits: "I want to make my marriage work."

And we can reveal Cheryl has met with England and Chelsea defender Ashley, 27, to talk things through. It was believed to have taken place in their country pile in Oxshott, Surrey, yesterday.

A source told us: "Chezza's been up and down but she's finally made her mind up. After meeting with Ashley, she told him in no uncertain terms that if he strays again, there will be no second chance.

"She told her band-mates on the way to the show that she was seeing Ashley the next day to tell him of her decision. The girls have been nothing but supportive but have been sworn to secrecy."

The 24-year-old Girls Aloud babe was devastated after her husband played away with hairdresser Aimee Walton. However, Cheryl was so nervous about her heart to heart with Ashley that she dramatically cut short her night at the Brits, sobbing: "I can't go on."

Constantly checking her mobile phone for text messages, the stony-faces singer broke down after being bombarded with questions about the state of her marriage from fellow guests at the star-studded bash.

SHE'S GOT THE X FACTOR

In 2008 her fame grew even bigger as she became a judge on the phenomenally successful ITV show 'The X Factor'. Girls Aloud still topped the charts and she also climbed Mount Kilimanjaro. Cheryl was well and truly on top of the world

FRICTION FACTOR

LOUIS WALSH STARTED the auditions on the back foot after being mocked by Cheryl. But he made her a star and has an eye for talent. Friends say he is keen to win again this year and will do anything to beat Cowell.

CHERYL COLE THE new girl passed her first day with flying colours and wasn't slow in coming forward. Chezza is already a hit with the male auditionees and they'll help take her mind off Ashley when she's out on the road.

DERMOT O'LEARY BACK fronting the show for a second series.

HOLLY WILLOUGHBY NEW face of ITV2's Xtra Factor spin-off

SIMON COWELL LIKE the cat who got the cream, Simon spent most of the day grinning and was looking at Dannii and Cheryl as much as the contestants. Hopes to find a genuine star this year like Leona Lewis.

DANNII MINOGUE AFTER winning the contest in her first year as a judge, Dannii is likely to be given a dodgy category this year and will find it harder to win again. Still, she can always rely on Cowell for a shoulder to cry on.

Growls aloud..

CHERYL LAYS INTO EX-BOSS AS JUDGES' BATTLE BEGINS

BY **MARK JEFFERIES**
mark.jefferies@mirror.co.uk

CHERYL Cole dived straight in to the X Factor bitching yesterday by calling fellow judge Louis Walsh a rubbish boss.

The Girls Aloud singer, 24, took the cheeky swipe at her ex-manager when a band began praising him at an audition.

A show source said: "The contestants said they wanted to have Louis as a boss and Cheryl piped up and joked 'No you don't'!"

"With a grin on her face she told them Louis was a rubbish manager - obviously in reference to when he was in charge of Girls Aloud.

"Other than that, the judges have been getting on well. There's lots of smiling and joking and Cheryl was playing her part and being

▶ **TEARS** Contestant Dominic Moone lets pressure get to him

vocal about the acts she liked and disliked."

Her taunting was a far cry from the shy girl who came into audition for Popstars: The Rivals six years ago when she was desperate to impress Louis. Months later he put her in Girls Aloud.

who clocked up a record 18 consecutive top 10 hits, before he stopped managing them two years ago to concentrate on his other bands and TV work.

Yesterday's auditions in London also saw lots of tears in front of the judging panel, which includes

Simon Cowell and Dannii Minogue. The very first act to go in front of them burst out crying when the big occasion got too much for him.

Dominic Moone, 19, needed 10 minutes to compose himself before he was able to return to the room to perform.

The source added: "We expected tears and tantrums here yet for once they weren't coming from the judges but the performers instead.

"It really is all smiles among the four judges... well it is for now anyway.

"Simon in particular seemed very happy and barely stopped grinning as he looked at Cheryl and Dannii sitting by his side."

POLLY HUDSON'S VERDICT

THE truly terrifying thing about this photo of the judges is that one assumes Dannii was trying to HIDE her true feelings. What a difference a series makes, eh? Last year Dannii was a rose between two thorns and a bitter old panto dame.

Seated in the middle, right next to Simon, dolled up to the nines and loving every second of the attention. Now she's firmly on the end of the panel, with flat hair, dead eyes, blatantly gritted teeth and not enough lip-gloss on.

Cheryl looks - as always - radiant, stunning, glowing and beyond beautiful. She'd probably just said something really, really funny just before the photo was taken, too.

Cowell looks like the cat who's got the cream and rightly so. Cheryl is a knockout addition to the judging panel who will breathe new life into the show.

The tension between the two female judges - Dannii called Girls Aloud chavs and they blanked her when they were on the show last year - will add a new dimension.

Round one definitely goes to Cheryl. Your move, Minogue...

Above: Ashley arrives in Manchester to surprise his wife on her 25th birthday, while she was recording The X Factor auditions. He brought flowers, balloons and a bag-shaped cake

Chezza's Angels
HEAVENLY 70s TV LOOK

HAIR BIG BOUFFANT WAVES GIVE CHERYL THAT PERFECT FARAH FAWCETT 'DO

VEST SKINNY PINK TOP CLINGS TO THIS ANGEL'S ASSETS IN ALL THE RIGHT PLACES

JEANS HIGH-WAISTED FLARES WITH A LEOPARD PRINT BELT TRULY ARE A ROARING SUCCESS

▶ **SO FARRAH, SO GOOD** Cheryl at X Factor auditions

By SARAH JELLEMA
s.jellema@mirror.co.uk

BIG hair, flared jeans and dazzling teeth... has Cheryl Cole joined Charlie's Angels?

The sexy singer, 24, turned up at X Factor auditions looking like she had stepped off the set of the glamorous 70s TV show.

Super-slim Cheryl had clearly been inspired by the styles of the series' icons Farrah Fawcett-Majors, Jaclyn Smith and Kate Jackson.

It was good to see Cheryl all smiles again after a relaxing beach break in the Costa del Sol with husband Ashley.

An onlooker said: "Cheryl definitely had superstar status when she stepped out of the car. She looked so good I bet everyone will be following her 70s style.

"Her wild hair was blowing about and she looked like she was in one of the show's slow-motion shots."

Cheryl joined fellow judges Simon Cowell, Dannii Minogue and Louis Walsh for the Birmingham round of the talent show's auditions on Monday.

With Cheryl and Dannii at his side, Simon has only to ditch one last wrinkly panellist before he has his very own dream set of X Factor Angels.

▲ **ON HOLS** With Ashley

▲ **BREEZING IN** With wild hair

▲ **DREAM TEAM** Charlie's Angels, from left, Kate, Jaclyn, Farrah in 1977

Pictures: STEVE WOODS/NEWSTEAM

Above: Cheryl adopts the Farah Fawcett look

Talon contest
Dannii v Cheryl – the gloves are off

Saturday, June 28, 2008

If you thought the atmosphere on the last X Factor was a bit frosty, be warned…the next one is set to be sub-Arctic.

New judge Cheryl Cole's only been there five minutes and the bitching, backstabbing and bickering has begun. Dannii Minogue – 12 years Cheryl's senior – has been walking round with a face like thunder.

A few days before this year's auditions were due to start, judge Sharon Osbourne quit after demanding a £1.25million pay rise.

And if Dannii – who fell out with Sharon before the series even started last year – thought all her Christmases had come at once, she was in for a shock.

Simon Cowell immediately hired Girls Aloud singer Cheryl to fill the gap.

On the surface, all was sweetness and light. "It's going to be great fun," gushed Dannii when the news was announced.

But just a fortnight later, the fun seems to have run out.

An insider says: "Dannii walked into Arsenal's Emirates Stadium for the auditions and you could tell she'd put in a lot of work into looking good. She knows there's a younger, more successful, more attractive kid on the block and they will both be fighting for attention.

"Dannii's face seems a lot tighter than last year and everyone is gossiping that she's had a bit of work done.

"She's 36 and Cheryl is just 24 and she's desperate not to be cast as the older Sharon Osbourne type – she wants to be Cheryl's equal. But it isn't working out like that.

"She's not happy that Cheryl is on £800,000, just £100,000 less than her. She feels there should be a bigger gap and, with Sharon gone, she should be earning nearer her £1.5m pay packet."

The stress of competing with Cheryl is starting to tell. After just a few days of filming the crew quickly got used to hearing Dannii complain about lighting, camera angles, catering and hotels.

Cheryl, meanwhile, has thrown herself into her new role with gusto. Just six years ago she was a Newcastle teenager dreaming of a life of stardom. She auditioned for Louis Walsh in Popstars: The Rivals and ended up joining Girls Aloud.

A stellar career followed that saw them become the most successful pop act in a decade, notching up 18 consecutive top 10 hits.

Little wonder that Dannii feels somewhat eclipsed.

And Cheryl has been a revelation in front of the camera. Our insider says: "She has a great empathy for those auditioning because she has been there herself.

"She has had a tough time and knows what it is like to go through this process. Simon is delighted with how things have gone.

"He is calling her the 'new Cilla Black'. She has that touch that connects with people. She is a natural fit to the show and makes Dannii somewhat redundant.

"Louis and Cheryl get on like a house on fire as he managed Girls Aloud. He has never really got on with Dannii so that has made her feel even more isolated.

"It's ironic that last year Sharon felt under threat from the younger rival when Dannii arrived. Now it is Dannii who is under pressure herself."

The last X Factor series saw a mediocre winner in Leon Jackson. But all the drama happened off stage as Sharon Osbourne was usurped by Dannii. A row between the two just before the first live show led to the pair barely speaking for the rest of the series.

Sharon told Graham Norton on his chat show: "She knows she is there because of her looks, not because of her contribution to the music industry."

At least no one can accuse Cheryl of lacking the right pop credentials. But despite her reputation as a tough cookie, the strains in her personal life have surfaced over the past fortnight.

She was devastated when her footballer husband Ashley, 27, was caught cheating with hairdresser Aimee Walton, 22.

The weight dropped off the already-slim star as Ashley begged for forgiveness. Before work began on the X Factor, Ashley whisked Cheryl off to Marbella for a holiday. But back in Britain, some auditions have seen Cheryl in floods of tears.

The insider says: "She says things are okay with Ashley when anyone asks. She has a reputation as a hard case but she has been in tears.

"The slightest thing can set her off – usually it is the young girls auditioning. I think she sees how she was herself once – when she was fresh and before the hurt Ashley has caused.

"It is obvious she is very upset about what's been happening but she's thrown herself into her new job. Seeing her sad and upset has made Simon and Louis very protective."

Above: Launching an official Girls Aloud book, 'Dreams That Glitter', in London, October 2008

A dazzling smile as she takes to the catwalk during a charity fashion show in London, September 2008

The £1m judge
Monday, September 29, 2008

X-Factor judge Cheryl Cole is being offered a 100 per cent rise by Simon Cowell to sign for next year's series.

But the TV mogul is racing against time to get the singer to agree to the £1m deal – as her band Girls Aloud are off to the USA.

A studio insider said: "Cheryl has been an instant hit with viewers and contestants. She initially signed a one-year deal as she wasn't sure how she would fare and Simon didn't want to commit to an unknown quantity. Now he's desperate to get her for a new series and put pen-to-paper.

"He realises he will have to fight to keep her as Girls Aloud are in talks to do a US tour.

"Simon needs to act fast and get her to sign before she has unavoidable commitments. As part of the package there's talk of involving her in another of Simon's shows. Cheryl is flattered."

Daily Mirror — MONDAY 13.10.2008

THE CHERYL COLE STORY

EXCLUSIVE BY CLARE RAYMOND
features@mirror.co.uk

IF anyone needed proof of how far Cheryl Cole has come, it was crystal clear for 11 million X Factor viewers on Saturday night.

Beaming from the plum seat next to Simon Cowell – where Dannii Minogue would love to be perched – Cheryl's first live X Factor show was a triumph.

Not only did she have the strongest acts, but her willingness to criticise Cowell conjured up memories of steely Sharon Osbourne. And if she stumbled over a couple of lines, it didn't spoil her night.

As fellow North-east girls Bad Lashes made their tearful departure, the glamorous life of multi-millionaire pop star Cheryl seemed a world away from the distraught wannabes.

And their sobs only served to underline the iron will that has taken Cheryl from a tough council estate to showbiz's top table.

As one of Girls Aloud, the most successful British girl band ever, the beauty has earnings of £5million and lives in a Surrey mansion with her chihuahua and soccer star husband Ashley Cole, worth £15million.

But Cheryl hasn't forgotten her own roots and how just six years ago she was one of those nervous teens trying to impress a panel of judges on Popstars: The Rivals.

And she has no intention of letting go of what she's got.

"I've wanted this for so long," she said. "If it ended, I think I'd shrivel into a ball."

Today, in the first of a landmark three-part series, we tell how the 25-year-old has got where she is thanks to the steely determination, ruthless ambition and relentless work ethic instilled in her during her tough working-class upbringing.

Growing up on a heroin-ridden estate in Heaton, Newcastle upon Tyne, Cheryl was a sensitive child who brought home injured pigeons and couldn't bear to watch horse racing because she thought it was cruel.

DRUGS

Her mum Joan, though, was quick to toughen her up and Cheryl said: "I remember me Mam once getting hold of me by both arms and shaking us, saying, 'This is ridiculous! There's a big bad world out there and you've got to toughen up'."

"My Mam would take me to auditions. If I got a part, Dad would shout, 'Get in there', but all Mum would say was, 'Oh, good.' She will always keep my feet on the ground."

And Cheryl could so easily have fallen into the sordid world of drugs.

"Heroin was there for the taking," she said. "I could easily have taken that route. That nightmare devastated family and friends."

She lost a close friend to heroin in 2005 and his mother agreed for his picture to be printed in newspapers as a warning to others. The needle was still in his arm.

"He was a talented boy who might have played for Newcastle," said Cheryl. "Where I come from everyone is exposed to drugs. I was strong enough to resist it."

When Girls Aloud eventually break up, she wants to set up a support network for addicts' families. But she added: "I don't have any sympathy for the addicts. That might sound harsh, but I don't give a f***. If they're in pain because of drugs, it's self-inflicted. You know what you're doing when you take it."

Born Cheryl Ann Tweedy on June 30, 1983, the future Mrs Cole showed a love of the limelight from an early age. She was named Bonniest Baby by the chemist Boots and won a children's modelling competition at six.

She went on to become the "Best Looking Girl of Newcastle" and "Most Attractive Girl" at a local shopping centre.

Joan stayed at home to raise Cheryl and her brothers Joseph, 32, Andrew, 28, Gary, 21, and sister Gillian, 29, while dad Gary worked as a painter and decorator.

And when, at the age of three, Cheryl demonstrated a love of music and dance, her family were right behind her. "There wasn't a lot of money but Mum and Dad always found enough for my audition outfits," said Cheryl. "I was the show-off in the family."

Joan recalled: "From the age of four she went to shopping centres all over the place, strutting her stuff on catwalks and stages. She has always wanted to be a star. She didn't want to do anything else. Nothing else would have satisfied her."

In 1990, when she was seven, she made an ad for British Gas in which she appeared in the bath with younger brother Gary.

At nine she dreamed of being a ballerina and was one of a handful of girls picked out of 5,000 to take part in the Royal Ballet School's two-week trial.

But she said: "I wanted to go home straight away. Everyone was prim and proper and I was a Geordie from a council estate. Their parents all had money and we struggled just to get the money to travel down to London. I was the odd one out." She cried every night

▲ **BONNY BAIRN** Cheryl at four

▲ **SWEET** Cheryl at the age of six

▲ **BALLERINA** But this fad did not last

▲ **TEEN SHOW-OFF** Cheryl was singing in public at 13

"There wasn't a lot of money but Mum and Dad always found it for my auditions"

▶ **SMILES** Cheryl and her mum

Making of the X Factor star

I've wanted this for so long.. if it ended now, I think I'd shrivel up into a ball

RIGHT AT HOME Cheryl with fellow X Factor judges Simon Cowell, Dannii Minogue and Louis Walsh

HOPEFUL With Davina McCall on Popstars: The Rivals

Cheryl in numbers

2002 year Girls Aloud was formed after winning Popstars: The Rivals

213,000 number of Sound of the Underground singles sold in the first week of release, which secured Girls Aloud the number 1 slot at Christmas 2002

18 consecutive Top 10 singles, which include three number ones and five platinum albums

£500,000 cost of Cheryl's wedding to Ashley Cole – but a magazine paid £1million to cover the day

GIRLS ALOUD Sarah, left, Nicole, Nadine, Cheryl, Kimberley

and decided she didn't want to be a dancer – but instead chose to pursue her love of singing. "It shattered my dream," she admitted. "But I didn't want to have to stand a certain way all my life and only eat salad."

At 10, she joined the Newcastle Dance Centre, doubling up with a boy partner for the British Dance Championships and performing on Michael Barrymore's My Kind of People. "I had to wear big bright pink or orange evening gowns, lots of make-up and sometimes even a tiara in those days," she laughed.

By the age of 12, she was signed up by a management company and she returned to the Dance Centre in her teens to have routines choreographed.

Then she started singing solo to shoppers at the MetroCentre in Gateshead.

But home life wasn't always happy. At 13, her brother Andrew started to get into trouble, leading to a criminal record of more than 70 offences, including robbery and attacking police. An alcoholic with an addiction to sniffing glue, he has also spent time behind bars for a vicious street mugging.

And while Cheryl shone at performing arts, she was never the brightest girl. "I was awful," she said. "They used to throw me out of class."

Her former headmaster at Newcastle's Walker Comprehensive, Dr Steve Gaiter, said: "It was obvious Cheryl was ambitious and talented. Her passions were singing and dancing. But we didn't anticipate how big she would become.

"She stood head and shoulders above everybody else. She loved being centre stage. Once she gave a speech to 250 kids for a Christmas box appeal and was so good that a letter of commendation was sent to her parents."

GROOMED

When she left school she found a job at JJ's cafe in Newcastle, where her flirty personality and curvy figure were a big hit with local builders.

She also worked as a £5-an-hour cocktail waitress on the River Tyne's floating nightclub Tuxedo Princess, as well as touring the pub and club circuit before auditioning for TV talent show Popstars: The Rivals in 2002.

With her fuller figure and high street clobber, she was far from the groomed, designer-clad woman we know today.

But her looks won over judges Geri Halliwell, Louis Walsh and Pete Waterman, who gushed after her first audition: "I think you have the most beautiful eyes and skin I've ever seen."

Cheryl was the first contestant to be picked for the all-girl line-up in the show hosted by Davina McCall. She was joined by Bradford's Kimberley Walsh, Manchester's Sarah Harding, Nadine Coyle from Derry and Runcorn's Nicola Roberts – and they became Girls Aloud.

And her rise to fully fledged popstar was complete that December when the band secured the Christmas No1 spot. Cheryl said: "Four months ago I was sitting in a council house drinking tea and watching Oprah Winfrey all day."

While their Popstars' co-winners, boy band One True Voice, fell apart after two singles, Girls Aloud became the most successful girl group in UK chart history, scoring 16 consecutive top 10s.

Cheryl has earned £3million from Girls Aloud, another million from deals and gets £800,000 as an X Factor judge.

"We've all grown into young women in the public eye," she said. "We are best friends. Looking back, I don't know how I lived without these girls."

But for Cheryl life was not always so easy when it came to men...

TOMORROW: CHERYL'S STEAMY SEX SECRETS

Above: The Daily Mirror tells the Cheryl story

Sat next to fellow X Factor judges Simon Cowell and Louis Walsh at the 2008 National Television Awards

The show is not about the judges (and that includes you too, Simon)

Saturday, November 22, 2008

As the darling of Saturday night TV, her career has gone stratospheric and life should be just peachy.

But not today…because X Factor judge Cheryl Cole is fuming. She's sick of the sideswipes, squabbling and egos which threaten to overshadow the show.

The Girls Aloud star is furious that the focus of the contest is all too often on which judge will emerge victorious.

In a blistering attack, Cheryl says the X Factor is not about her, Dannii Minogue or Louis Walsh.

It's not even – gasp! – about Simon Cowell.

In an exclusive interview with the Mirror, she rages: "It really p***** me off. This isn't about me, Louis, whatever. No! None of the judges are going to win it. People don't vote for the judges. They vote for their favourite contestant.

"Diana Vickers or Alexandra Burke will win it, not us. We're there to judge, to give advice, to build relationships with them.

"Of course, if one of my girls wins I'm going to go through the roof. But not because I've won. And I promise you I'm going to make damned sure one of my girls wins."

Fighting talk from X Factor's newest (and feistiest) judge. But with Geordie Cheryl's own experience on Popstars: The Rivals back in 2002, it's little wonder she feels so passionate.

She says: "No one else on the panel knows how it feels to be stood on that stage. They don't understand what it's like to be so young and have 12 million people watching you sing live every Saturday. What an immense amount of pressure."

Since joining the X Factor team she's become the nation's new sweetheart, charming viewers with her warmth, humility, steely commitment, tears, smiles and wit.

Men fancy her. Women adore her. Cheryl, it seems, can do no wrong.

The problems which caused her so much grief at the start of 2008 seem to be behind her. Chelsea star husband Ashley is a fixture in the X Factor audience every Saturday and Cheryl has made it clear it's time to move on.

Cheryl is dressed down in high-waisted flared jeans, with neck-breaking heels. Her make-up is immaculate, her hair tumbles around her tiny shoulders, her eyes sparkle and her smile is genuine. She's slim, yet doesn't look unhealthily skinny. There's no denying it – Cheryl is devastatingly beautiful.

It's been nearly six years since she, Kimberley, Sarah, Nadine and Nicola pipped rival reality boyband One True Voice to the Christmas No. 1 slot with their debut single, 'Sound of the Underground'.

Since then, they've notched up four No. 1 singles. All 19 of their singles have reached the top 10. 'Out of Control', their fifth studio album and sixth overall, shot straight to No. 1.

Next year sees them embark on another UK arena tour and they have a credibility most of the other pop bands would kill for.

"We have to pinch ourselves," says Cheryl. "We're ordinary girls. We've only been able to afford designer clothes in the last couple of years. The ticket sales for the tour have been incredible. Newcastle sold out within half-an-hour.

"The songs have given us credibility. We came into the industry with a fresh sound and we've stayed true to that. The fans have stayed true, too, which is fantastic."

Cheryl at the 2008 Daily Mirror Pride of Britain Awards, where she caught the attention of then Prime Minister Gordon Brown. Above, she joins Nicola and Kimberley on stage to present a Child of Courage award to Levana Hanson

Girls Aloud perform and accept the award for Best British Single at the 2009 Brits. On the opposite page, Cheryl is centre stage while singing the song during the ceremony

The four fashion

By AMBER MORALES
Fashion Director

WHAT a whirlwind seven years it's been for Cheryl Cole. From Geordie wannabe on Pop Stars: The Rivals in 2002, to Girls Aloud chart-topper, WAG wife at the World Cup, to A-list judge on the X Factor. Here's how her style has changed...

THE WANNABE YEARS 2002-2004

IN 2002, a 19-year-old Newcastle lass called Cheryl Tweedy belted out S Club 7's Have You Ever at the Pop Stars: The Rivals audition and by the end of the year was at No1 with Sound of the Underground with her Girls Aloud pals.

Those early fashion days left a lot to be desired – a pink ruffle cowboy-style shirt, ill-fitting jeans for her audition, then a shocking combats and heels combo with fake fur gilet to Chinawhite nightclub.

A year later, at the Legally Blonde 2 Premiere, things were no better in a dodgy ripped black dress with pink belt.

THE WAG YEARS 2005-2006

LOVED up with soccer star Ashley Cole, Cheryl's fashion muse quickly became her fellow WAG Victoria Beckham, her style shadow during the World Cup in Baden Baden in 2006.

So bring on the hair extensions, fake tan, long nails, maxi dresses, and hotpants. And who can forget that incredibly cheesy Lottery ad in July 2006 in that white ruffled dress?

ages of Cheryl Cole

THE SUPERSTYLED YEARS 2006-2007

▶ September 2006 heralded a new era for the newlywed Mrs Cheryl Cole.
Styled to within an inch of her life, she stunned everybody by turning up at the Versace dinner with a sleek fresh hairstyle and polished new look.
In November, she stole the show in a stylish strapless prom dress at fellow band member Kimberley Walsh's birthday. By 2007, she was a fashion-forward style icon — becoming the first celeb to wear a Herve Leger bandage dress at a Samsung phone launch.

THE POST-STYLIST YEARS 2008-2009

▶ BY 2008, Cheryl was confident enough to know her own taste. And while hiring stylists for her X Factor and other TV appearances, she began experimenting with hot new designers such as Alexander Wang and developing her own, edgier look.
For last month's X Factor auditions, she mix-matched blue and red in an Alexander McQueen tulip skirt and an 80s-inspired top.
On Wednesday night, she became more daring than ever for her 26th birthday party in a peekaboo £4,000 Alexander McQueen dress, with Christian Louboutin peep toes and a Furla bag.
In Manchester yesterday she teamed a cute bow mini-skirt with a daring stripey top.

Climbing celebs say high to Gord

Friday, March 13, 2009

Comic Relief's celebrity Kilimanjaro heroes scaled new heights yesterday — at 10 Downing Street.

The stars who climbed Africa's highest peak met Gordon Brown to discuss a £2million donation to fight malaria in Tanzania.

Over afternoon tea, the PM congratulated Cheryl Cole, Kimberley Walsh, Gary Barlow, Alesha Dixon and the others for raising more than £1.5million.

Mr Brown said: "Comic Relief shows us Britain is filled with people willing to go the extra mile to help somebody else."

Left: Another meeting with Gordon Brown, this time on 10 Downing Street, after Cheryl joined a group of celebrities including Alesha Dixon, Kimberley Walsh and Gary Barlow, in climbing Mount Kilimanjaro for Comic Relief

CHERYL

GOING SOLO

Within the space of a few months Cheryl broke out on her own in more ways than one. She released her first solo album and enjoyed a number one single. Then she ended her marriage to cheating husband Ashley Cole. Still, she's not short of admirers

Cheryl's got the Jay-Z factor

Tuesday, November 11, 2009

Christmas has come early for Cheryl Cole. She's gone platinum in the UK and now she won't have to Fight Fight Fight to make it in the US.

We can reveal that the richest man in hip-hop, Jay-Z, wants to take the X Factor judge under his wing and kick-start her career stateside.

The pair are in talks for a collaboration and Cheryl is over the moon.

She already has the backing of US hit-maker will.i.am, who produced her debut album 3 Words. Now she's hoping to make music with Beyonce's hubby too.

We're told: "Cheryl's the biggest fan of Jay-Z and Beyonce. To hear the feeling is mutual has totally made her year.

"She never imagined her album would have taken off like this. To get Jay-Z's support is beyond her wildest dreams."

It all came about after Chezza hit it off with Beyonce on X Factor.

After Bey's tear-jerking duet with Cheryl's contestant Alexandra Burke last year, the girls hung out in the dressing rooms – and it has certainly paid off.

Above: Performing her first solo single, 'Fight For This Love', at the BBC Children In Need Rocks concert at the Royal Albert Hall, November 2009
Right: A wave to the audience during the Children In Need show

CHERYL

With fellow Geordie Joe McElderry, who she mentored to victory in the 2009 X Factor, at The Sage Gateshead, a North-East music venue

Joe and the Daily Mirror, the day after his victory

Rock 'n' Cole

KECKS FACTOR Cheryl poses in spiky top and slashed leather jeans

ON ASHLEY..
He talks to me about football but I don't really understand the tactical side of it.

ON CAMERON..
Slippery, isn't he? We've always been Labour in our family – it feels wrong not to be.

ON GIRLS ALOUD..
The other day I was like, 'Why go solo when I have four friends as a security blanket?'

EXCLUSIVE
BY **TOM BRYANT**
tom.bryant@mirror.co.uk

NEW-LOOK CHERYL ALL REVVED UP

CHERYL Cole takes a walk on the wild side in her latest sizzling photoshoot.

The chart-topping singer and X Factor judge ditches her normally laid-back style for a sexy rock chick look, complete with skin-tight leathers.

And feisty Cheryl, 26, also delivers a biker-style bashing to David Cameron.

The Tory leader has described her as the "most fanciable" member of Girls Aloud. But asked what she thought of HIM, Cheryl shivered and said: "David Cameron. Brrrrr. Slippery isn't he?" She added: "We've always been Labour in our family, it just feels wrong not to be. Better the devil you know."

In an interview with Q magazine, Cheryl also gave a glimpse of what it's like to live with her ultra competitive husband, Chelsea and England star Ashley, 29. She says: "He hates losing. He talks to me about football, but I don't really understand the tactical side of it." And she revealed that deep down Ashley is "ridiculously, painfully shy".

Cheryl confirmed she got a 100 per cent pay rise after her first series on X Factor, saying: "Can't complain about that."

She also hit out at rumours that she's all set to turn her back on her Girls Aloud bandmates to go solo full-time.

She said: "I can't be out there alone. I'm not at that point yet. The other day I was like, 'Oh God, why would you even do this when you've got four friends as a security blanket?"

▶ **Q Magazine is out December 27**

▲ **SLEEK** In sexy clinging outfit

Pictures: JOHN WRIGHT/Q MAGAZINE

LLOYD ROCKS SCREAMING FANS: PAGE 15

Above: A rock chick photoshoot for Q magazine

Walking up to the stage after The X Factor was named Most Popular Talent Show at the National Television Awards

CHERYL

Hot 'n' Cole

Wednesday, February 17, 2010

Brave Cheryl Cole hid her heartache to wow a star-studded audience at last night's Brit Awards.

The supercool singer gave a gutsy performance in the wake of the latest revelations over her footballer husband Ashley's alleged cheating.

Just hours before going on stage, onlookers said Geordie Cheryl, 26, appeared "red-eyed and close to tears" and just wanted to be left alone.

But she emerged triumphant after vowing: "Nothing's going to ruin my big night."

After she strutted sexily around the stage to her hit track 'Fight For This Love', host Peter Kay told the audience: "Gotta fight for this love. Never a truer word said."

At the end of the set, some fans chanted: "Dump him! Dump him!" in an apparent reference to Ashley.

But Cheryl seemed unfazed and just kept mouthing the words "thank you".

As she left the stage she was hugged by band-mates Kimberley Walsh and Nicola Roberts, who had been waiting in the wings.

Earlier yesterday a rumour spread that Cheryl was set to pull out of the show. It came after England star Ashley was accused of twice sneaking a blonde secretary into Chelsea's team hotel for trysts in his room.

Cheryl was already reeling after naked pictures of the England star were allegedly sent to glamour model Sonia Wild.

But sources close to the singer last night insisted that she "never, ever" considered scrapping her performance in light of the claims. One insider said: "She won't let anything get in the way of her big night. She is focused and just wants to enjoy the moment."

Above and left: Performing solo at the 2010 Brits, while the saga of her marriage breakdown is played out publically (right)

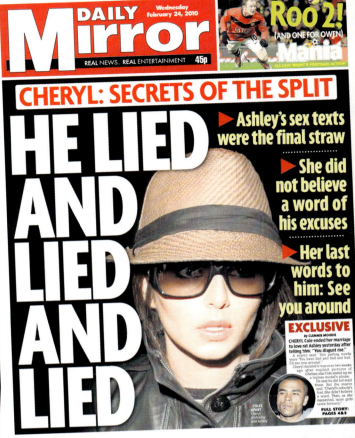

CHERYL

Cheryl needy

Monday, April 5, 2010

Hunky Derek Hough has visited Cheryl Cole as he continues to comfort her following her split from Ashley Cole.

Dancer Derek, 24, arrived at her West Hollywood bolthole at 10am on Saturday and left two hours later.

A source close to Cheryl said: "They hung out and get on very well. It is just a platonic friendship but he's been a massive support."

Cheryl, 26, who has been working non-stop on new tracks in the US, later visited Simon Cowell for dinner on Saturday night.

The source added: "Cheryl saw Derek on a break from her busy schedule. She has been working her socks off and was relieved to have some time off to see her friends."

The dancer, from Utah, who is paired with Nicole Scherzinger on Dancing With The Stars, has asked her to come along as his guest of honour at the glittering live show today.

Derek, who performed on the video for her single '3 Words', comforted Cheryl at another LA hotel in February after she flew out following her Brits performance.

It was after she arrived back in Britain that she announced her decision to separate from husband Ashley.

Getting cosy with will.i.am at an after-show party

Will.i.only have eyes for Cheryl

Friday, May 7, 2010

Ashley who? Cheryl Cole is sooo over her love-rat hubby if her antics at the Black Eyed Peas' after-party are anything to go by.

We looked on in amazement as Chezza cosied up to head Pea will.i.am, whispering in his ear, sharing text messages and getting down on the dancefloor.

And just to seal the deal, she even introduced him to her mum at an after-show party.

We were among the lucky few to get into the exclusive Bacardi VIP area at London's Indigo O2 on Wednesday night.

Will, 35, turned up first at midnight and came over for a chat. He said: "High five, girls. I love London girls, so hot. And Cheryl is so sexy, come on now."

He didn't have to wait long for his favourite lady to arrive.

Cheryl – who opened for the band at their O2 gig – was ushered in with four minders just after midnight. With no wedding ring on her finger, the 26-year-old Girls Aloud babe has never looked happier. She told us: "Thank you so much for coming. I can't believe I've done the show. Thank you."

Cheryl was then whisked to Will's table, which was packed with champers, Bacardi mojitos, daiquiris and a special VIPea cocktail.

After a couple of drinks it was time for the A-list pair to throw some shapes on the dancefloor.

It was Cheryl's first big night out since her split with Chelsea ace Ashley and she was determined to make the most of it.

She left the rapper drooling with her sexy dance moves, writhing her tiny waist and wiggling her hips.

At one point Will jumped on the sofa to serenade her using his bottle opener as a microphone to belt out 'Sex On Fire'. Oo-er!

Then when his No. 1 hit 'OMG' came on, Cheryl put down her mojito and pretended to bow down to him.

It's not the first time will.i.am has gone public about his feelings for Cheryl.

Earlier in the evening, during the Black Eyes Peas' wild AEG Live The End tour, Will launched into an impromptu rap which included the lyrics: "Cheryl Cole, will you marry me?"

And later on at the party he even got the chance to meet Cheryl's mum, when Joan joined them for a boogie.

Like mother, like daughter, eh…

Getting up close with Derek Hough while performing at Wembley

Chezza gets in a Hough

Saturday, May 29, 2010

Cheryl Cole secretly flew in hunky dancer Derek Hough to join her on tour in the UK – just days after filing for divorce from Ashley Cole.

She got Derek up on stage at the 02 Arena last night – sending a very public message to her soon-to-be-ex-hubby.

The pair enjoyed a steamy ballroom dance during Cheryl's performance of her hit single 'Parachute' at the London venue.

She said at the end: "Ladies and gentleman, Mr Derek Hough."

Cheryl then blew him a kiss. Cheeky.

A source tells us: "If ever there was a clearer statement that she's over her ex, this is it. Derek has always been very supportive of Cheryl."

Derek, 24, provided a shoulder to cry on when the Girls Aloud babe flew to Los Angeles in the immediate aftermath of her split from Ashley in February.

The American spent almost 10 hours with Cheryl, 26, in her suite in Hollywood's London Hotel following claims that Ashley, 29, had betrayed her by bedding four girls and exchanging explicit pictures with a fifth. Derek, who Cheryl has described as a "sweetheart", finally left at 4.15am.

Then in April, while she was on a recording trip, he was seen visiting her West Hollywood hotel for two hours.

Apparently, Cheryl was desperate for Derek to join her on her current tour after he finished his stint on US TV show Dancing with The Stars. He flew from LA via New York to London on Thursday, and has been holed up in a luxury five-star hotel.

A source says: "Cheryl was really excited about seeing Derek again. He has been a real rock for her and a real breath of fresh air to be around. She is so pleased that he has found time in his busy schedule to be there for her."

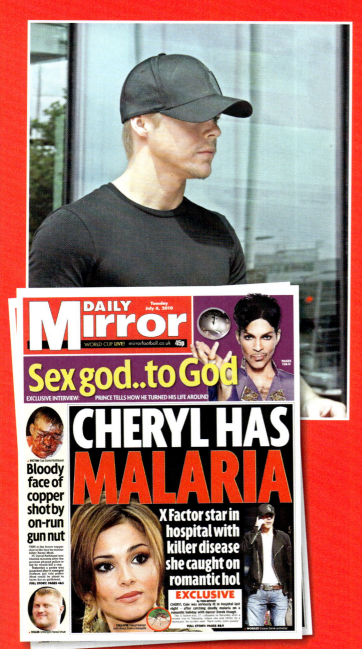

She's Cole-axed

Tuesday, July 6, 2010

Cheryl Cole's close friend Derek Hough was said to be devastated last night – as she lay seriously ill in hospital battling malaria.

The dancer is distraught after being told she caught the deadly disease on a romantic break that he arranged for them.

Doctors believe Cheryl was bitten by a mosquito in Tanzania where she and Derek spent six days together last month.

A source said: "He's mortified by what's happened and is utterly devastated at what she's going through – not least because it happened on a trip he'd planned."

Derek, 25, has been at the Geordie singer's bedside since she was admitted to London's private Cromwell hospital on Sunday evening.

Shocked Cheryl, 27, was diagnosed with malaria when she went for urgent tests after collapsing at a photoshoot on Saturday.

One insider said: "She just got worse and worse after Saturday and was taken in by her worried management team as it became clear she wasn't getting any better.

"She really is quite poorly but at least the results came back quickly so the doctors can focus on giving her the right treatment.

"She had been taking malaria tablets regularly while on holiday and continued to take them even after she returned, but she still tested positive for it."

Cheryl is expected to be kept in for at least three nights while she is treated for the disease, which kills between one and three million people a year, mainly in Africa.

She is almost certain to miss this weekend's X Factor auditions in Manchester. Fellow judge Simon Cowell contacted Cheryl yesterday and told her: "I don't want to see you back until you are well enough. Just rest and concentrate on getting better."

A show source said: "The situation will be reviewed on a day-by-day basis, but obviously Cheryl's health comes first."

Insiders slammed reports she was suffering from exhaustion, saying that Cheryl was a "tough cookie" and used to hard work.

The source said: "All this stuff about Cheryl burning the candle at both ends and working too hard is just absolute nonsense. Cheryl always operates at a million miles an hour; in fact, she thrives on it.

"It's such a shame as she had such a lovely holiday with Derek and has such lovely memories of it. He is worried sick about her. He's sticking close by her bedside and trying to keep her cheerful.

"He's probably the best tonic she's got right now."

Derek had whisked Cheryl to Tanzania for an idyllic break after she told him she had fallen in love with it following her Comic Relief climb up Mount Kilimanjaro last year.

Cheryl is named Woman of the Year at the Glamour Awards in June

EXCLUSIVE

Derek ..the truth

he makes my days enjoyable. I'm slowly finding my feet

"It's a very different feeling being out there on your own. Slowly but surely I'm finding my feet. It was scary and exciting at the same time, but definitely felt the right thing to do"

Right: Cheryl speaks about Derek Hough, who was at her side when she fell ill with malaria in summer 2010

CHERYL'S STORY: DAY 1

BY JULIE McCAFFREY
features@mirror.co.uk

NEW MAN Cheryl with Derek Hough

> I've had the craziest past couple of years. Who knows what's in store?
> **CHERYL COLE**

HOLDING a vodka cranberry aloft as she dined with close friends, Cheryl Cole drank a toast to "moving on".

That dinner, in London's posh Japanese restaurant Sumosan after a long day of X Factor filming, was only a few days ago. But her vow to make a fresh start was made weeks before as she lay in hospital recovering from near-fatal malaria.

Facing death, and enduring the pain of divorce, has made the past eight months the worst of Cheryl's life. But they are exactly that – the past.

Now, on the brink of signing a new £3million deal with Simon Cowell to become a judge on the American version of X Factor, it's clear the nation's sweetheart is focusing firmly on her future.

Next month sees the launch of her second solo album, Messy Little Raindrops, and the X Factor live finals.

Separating from serial cheat Ashley Cole has made her sexier. Singing without the back-up of Girls Aloud has made her a stronger performer. And the new man in her life, dancer Derek Hough, has made Cheryl happier. In her new book Through My Eyes, serialised across 21 pages of Hello!, the stunning star explains her trepidation and excitement about stepping into the spotlight alone.

Cheryl, 27, says: "It's a very different feeling being out there on your own. Slowly but surely I'm finding my feet.

"It was scary and exciting at the same time, but definitely felt the right thing to do."

After a tumultuous year of career highs and personal lows, Cheryl has changed.

Hurt and humiliated by the husband she loved, she has decided not to dwell on past pain but to learn hard lessons and move forward. Asked if she feels betrayed by Chelsea and England footballer Ashley, Cheryl says: "Yes, definitely I do. But I've got to take everything that's happened and learn from it. I accept that's a chapter of my life that's finished. And I've just got to be grateful that there are so many good things going on."

Derek, 25, is the perfect antidote to Ashley. A world champion in ballroom and Latin, he shares a passion for dance with Cheryl who, at the age of nine, beat 9,000 hopefuls for a place at the Royal Ballet School.

SWEETHEART

He is sensitive, caring and loyal. Cheryl says: "Derek is a sweetheart, the kind of person who makes the day more enjoyable. And that's really important when you're on a set doing a video for 18, 19 hours – maybe longer."

Whether the pair are lovers or just loving friends remains to be seen. But Cheryl, who looks as immaculate as her L'Oreal adverts every day, will never be short of male admirers.

Black Eyed Peas singer Will.i.am made no secret of his crush on her, gushing: "She's the prettiest, hottest girl. I'd move to London if it meant being with her."

True to his word, the rapper dropped work on his album to "jump on the next plane" and be by Cheryl's side when she asked for his help judging X Factor contestants.

And show insiders said their touchy-feely body language hinted at more than just friendship. Show sources also say Cheryl will quit X Factor after this year's series for the Stateside version.

Such a high profile stint on US prime-time TV will send her fame and fortune stratospheric.

Thanks to the constant support of her close-knit and ultra-protective team of friends and colleagues, including manager Hilary Shaw, PA Lily England and hair and make-up expert Lisa Laudat, the down-to-earth Geordie's feet will remain solidly on the ground.

But the one person she loves and trusts more than any other is her mum and constant companion, Joan Callaghan. Cheryl says: "She's the most grounded person..I can be hysterical and she's like 'Calm down, what's wrong with you?' She's absolutely brilliant if I'm feeling the pressure."

After such a life-changing year, Cheryl has matured immensely. Interviews are rarer, more guarded and are no longer spent embroiled in celebrity spats with the likes of Charlotte Church, Lily Allen, Ulrika Jonsson or Pete Doherty.

Breaking from Girls Aloud bandmates Nicola Roberts, 24, Kimberley Walsh, 28, Sarah Harding, 28, and Nadine Coyle, 25, has also made Cheryl more calm and confident on and off stage. She says: "On tour with Girls Aloud it was quite chaotic before a show.

"On my own, I've learned to prepare in a different way by putting on my headphones and zoning out."

Cheryl's bleak time in intensive care has taught her never to take her health for granted.

Despite one of the most punishing schedules in showbiz, she tries to get more than her typical four hours' sleep a night by taking daytime naps, and frequently sips peppermint tea as part of her health kick.

Future goals for one of the most eligible women in the world include becoming a mother.

Cheryl says: "That's definitely something I want to achieve. It's the toughest job in the world, but I know it must be the most rewarding too."

For now, though, Cheryl is too busy, happy and successful with her career to consider putting it on hold.

She declares: "I would never want to give up what I do. I love my music, I love being a judge on X Factor.

"I've had the craziest past couple of years ever. Who knows what's in store for me in the future?"

ASH & ME..THE BREAKDOWN

CHERYL has been freed to pursue her dream of US stardom by the end of her marriage to Ashley Cole.

She is no longer restricted by the demands of his football career.

But it had all seemed so perfect at first. The popstar and premiership footballer falling in love was like Posh and Becks all over again. Cheryl Tweedy and Ashley Cole started dating in October 2004 and, after only three months, he told her he loved her.

Cheryl says: "He just said it before his brain caught up. 'I f****** love you'." Less than one year later he went down on one knee on holiday in Dubai and popped the question. She reveals: "It was honestly the happiest moment of my life."

They married in July 2006 – but the honeymoon period was shortlived. In January 2008, she was rocked by revelations he had cheated on her with hairdresser Aimee Walton, 22. She vowed at the time: "We are in love. I won't let this woman destroy our marriage."

Sadly, that was not the last of Ashley's cheating. This year he sent illicit pictures of himself to model Sonia Wild. Three other women, Liverpool FC secretary Vikki Gough, US political aide Anne Corbitt and topless model Alexandra Taylor, then claimed to have had liaisons with him. It was the final straw.

> When he proposed, it was the happiest moment of my life
> **CHERYL ON ASHLEY**

TOMORROW: Her journey from pop wannabe to national treasure

Signing a copy of her new book, 'Through My Eyes', October 2010

Launching a luxury jewellery range she designed with de Grisogono at Nobu restaurant in London, September 2010